NOTTINGHAM
IN OLD PHOTOGRAPHS
1944–1974

SEVERN'S, MIDDLE PAVEMENT in 1967, just prior to its demolition. Efforts were made to save this small fifteenth-century building and it was rebuilt on Castle Road.

NOTTINGHAM
IN OLD PHOTOGRAPHS
1944–1974

COLLECTED BY
DOUGLAS WHITWORTH

ALAN SUTTON
Published in collaboration with

Alan Sutton Publishing Limited
Phoenix Mill · Far Thrupp · Stroud · Gloucestershire

First Published 1991
Reprinted 1992, 1993

British Library Cataloguing in Publication Data

Nottingham in old photographs 1944–1974.
I. Whitworth, Douglas, *1927–*
942.527

ISBN 0-86299-973-1

Typeset in 9/10 Korinna.
Typesetting and origination by
Alan Sutton Publishing Limited.
Printed in Great Britain by
The Bath Press, Avon.

CONTENTS

DEDICATION: To my wife, Margaret.

CORONATION PARTY IN HYSON GREEN, 1953. This was probably the last occasion on which street parties were held in Nottingham and, although the weather was not too kind, everyone appears to be enjoying themselves.

PARK STEPS, which lead down from The Ropewalk to Park Valley, has always had an attraction for photographers and children.

INTRODUCTION

Nottingham has changed considerably since the end of the Second World War – not always, in my opinion, for the better; and even now the planners have new schemes to alter the two shopping centres and change the centre of the city again.

These photographs, taken in Nottingham since the last year of the Second World War, are an attempt to show some of the events that have taken place in the subsequent thirty years and to act as a reminder of the scenes and building of that period.

We were more fortunate than many other provincial cities in not suffering too heavily from German bombing so the Nottingham Corporation had no need to plan and rebuild with any great urgency. Changes did take place eventually though, and in the 1960s a major road – Maid Marian Way – was built from Chapel Bar to Canal Street and many interesting buildings and streets disappeared, including the Collin's Almshouses on Friar Lane, which caused a storm of protest.

Further east, when the Broad Marsh Shopping Centre was built, Drury Hill, the road to London in the Middle Ages, was submerged in the building. Many architecturally interesting factories and warehouses in the Lace Market were demolished during this period without sufficient forethought being given, until it was eventually realized that the area was being ruined, and sympathetic building and restoration is now taking place.

Other districts, such as Sneinton, St Ann's and the Meadows have been the subject of major rebuilding, leaving pockets of older houses which were worth retaining and restoring.

The Victoria Shopping Centre was the first of its kind to be built in the country – on the site of the Victoria railway station. These centres changed the shopping habits of Nottingham people and some of the larger stores in the city centre either moved into one of the shopping precincts or eventually closed down, Pearson Bros being the most recent.

Post-war Nottingham was a prosperous city with varied industries. Boots, the subject of a section of this book, was still basically a pharmaceutical and toiletries concern with a retail shop in almost every main street in town. Raleigh Cycles were world famous and, as the age of the car for almost every family had not yet arrived, the home market was very strong. John Player had not yet diversified, but the market for cigarettes was enormous and to work at Player's seemed to be the ultimate achievement for Nottingham people.

The coal industry was also booming and, besides many coal mines to the north of the city, there were still pits within the city boundaries, such as Radford and

MALT MILL LANE, BROAD MARSH in October 1945. The street remains, but the atmosphere of this photograph has vanished.

Clifton collieries. However, as they became uneconomic they were closed and a new colliery was opened at Cotgrave to replace them.

Ericsson Telephones, now GPT, although outside the city, employed many hundreds of Nottingham men and women, as did British Rail. Besides these major employers there were hundreds of smaller concerns all contributing towards making Nottingham a thriving city.

It was at one of these smaller businesses, J. Hardy and Co. Ltd, general wholesalers in St James's Street, that I started work in 1941. My employers were running a delivery pool among local wholesalers to conserve petrol and, as office junior, I had to carry messages to other firms in the Lace Market and Hounds Gate area thereby acquiring a very good knowledge of the streets and alleys of Nottingham.

Maypole Yard was one such passage, which disappeared when the Black Boy Hotel was cruelly demolished to make way for a department store. Other narrow thoroughfares, now altered or closed, include Spaniel Row, the West End Meat Market and the passage from St James's Street to Angel Row by the side of the Odeon Cinema, where a glimpse could be had of the garden of Bromley House. The Beatles emerged from the Odeon Cinema into this alley after a concert in the 1960s in an attempt to escape the attentions of their fans.

I started taking photographs in 1942 when film was very difficult to obtain and I had to cultivate the friendship of local chemists in an attempt to buy it. One such chemist, Mr Scattergood of Woodborough Road, was always sure he would have supplies the following week but I cannot remember them arriving.

I bought an Olympus Miniature camera in April 1945 and, luckily, I managed to obtain some ex-RAF film and was able to take photographs in the Old Market Square on VE Day. People listening to Mr Churchill's speech to the nation announcing the end of the war in Europe, broadcast over loudspeakers, were fairly sober in manner although there was dancing and singing later on. As double summer time was then in operation the Council House was not illuminated until rather late in the evening, but crowds stayed on and we all walked home, the ATS girls singing alternative versions of popular songs.

I belonged to the Nottingham and Notts. Photographic Society at that time and young members were encouraged to take pictorial views, but these did not interest me too much and I preferred photographing people and events. In the next ten years I took hundreds of photographs, not only in Nottingham but also in London and Paris.

The Quincentenary, in 1949, which has a section devoted to it, was the five hundredth anniversary of the granting of the Great Charter by Henry VI, which made Nottingham a county in its own right. The celebrations included a royal visit by Princess Elizabeth and the Duke of Edinburgh, exhibitions, pageants, sporting events, fireworks, and a Nottingham Symphony composed by Alan Bush.

Several of the photographs in these pages will revive memories for older readers of the cafés and restaurants in Nottingham in the immediate post war years. Both Kardomah and Capoccis had several cafés in the city and other well-known cafés were Lloyds Coffee House in Bridlesmith Gate where they sold delicious cream cakes, the Oriental Café in Wheeler Gate, the Mikado Café on Long Row, King's Restaurant on Beastmarket Hill and Severn's on Middle Pavement.

Some of the grocery shops of high repute at that time were Burton's and Skinner and Rook; also well known were Marsden's, Home and Colonial and Lipton's, none of which have survived. Among the high-class confectioners in the city were Champkin's, Buol's, Meldrum's and Croshaw's, sadly only memories now.

Cinemagoers had a much greater choice in that era. Among cinemas in the centre of town were the Ritz, now the Odeon, the Carlton, later renamed Cannon, the Elite, Scala, Mechanics, New Victoria and the Hippodrome, later the Gaumont.

Sport is also covered and will evoke memories of Nottingham's cricket and football teams after the war. Some of the most exciting days for Notts. County were in the late 1940s and early '50s when the legendary Tommy Lawton played for the club. He drew huge crowds and high scoring games were frequent. Unfortunately, Notts. County only reached the Second Division during Lawton's time with the club, and following his departure the team suffered a slow decline until the 1970s.

Nottingham Forest, under Billy Walker's management, were finally promoted to the First Division in 1957 and won the FA Cup two years later in a classic game of football. Although the team remained in the First Division until 1972, their only successful season was 1966/7 when they finished second in the league.

At Trent Bridge, while the county cricket team never won any championships, some of the great players of the time appeared in test matches. Don Bradman came in 1948 along with Keith Miller, Ray Lindwall, Lindsey Hassett and others, and in 1950, when the West Indies came with Frank Worrell, Everton Weekes and Clyde Walcott, huge queues formed outside the ground waiting to gain admission to the test match.

The Festival of Britain was one of the highlights of the 1950s but, apart from Trowell surprisingly being designated the Festival village, it did not have the same impact in Nottingham as the Quincentenary.

In 1953 Nottingham, like other towns and cities, celebrated the coronation of Queen Elizabeth II with parades and pageants, but those with long memories will remember it as the first major event they witnessed on television – probably in a neighbour's house, on a 9 inch screen.

The 1960s was the decade in which Nottingham's planners debated the future of the city, and following the closure of the Victoria station in 1967 the area was cleared for the second time in seventy years, this time to build the Victoria Centre. At the same time, in an effort to draw traffic away from the city centre, the Broad Marsh Shopping Centre was built on undeveloped land at Broad Marsh.

My own photographs of Nottingham, taken between 1944 and the completion of the two shopping precincts in 1974, form the basis for this book, but the work of two other local photographers, Frank Stevenson and John Lock is also represented.

Frank Stevenson, who died in 1964, devoted most of his adult life to photographing Nottinghamshire, first as an amateur and then as a *Nottingham Journal* and *Nottingham Evening News* photographer. He was awarded the Associateship of the Royal Photographic Society, a testament to his artistry and photographic skills. Some of his very early bromoil prints, still in existence after seventy years, show his outstanding ability. A collection of his work was published in a book by Ralph Gee, a splendid tribute to his art. Frank Stevenson's daughters,

Mrs May Sentance and Miss Dorothy Stevenson, have fortunately saved his huge collection of plates and prints, together with his cameras and equipment, and have kindly allowed me to use some of his photographs.

John Lock has also been a photographer since his youth and some of his fine pictures are reproduced here. He has had the foresight to record many Nottingham buildings which have now disappeared. Besides his many photographs he has a large and varied collection of Nottingham memorabilia and artefacts, and his gift of Boots historical material was the basis of the present Boots museum.

The thirty years following the Second World War, covered by this personal view of Nottingham, were a great opportunity for the civic authorities to plan and build a better city. I feel that opportunity was missed for, although some changes were for the better, such as the building of Clifton Bridge and the rebuilding of St Ann's and the Meadows, many fine buildings were demolished, to be replaced mainly by faceless shopping centres, dual carriageways and multi-storey offices and car parks. The city authorities are now aware of Nottingham's heritage and are making determined efforts to redress the previous mistakes and are following a policy of conserving the best of Nottingham's past without sacrificing its future.

CLIFTON COLLIERY after its closure in April 1969 when it had become uneconomic. This colliery, which was opened in 1870, was the first to be nationalized, in 1943.

THEATRE SQUARE in December 1959. The old-style Theatre Royal hoarding advertises Jimmy Jewel and Ben Warriss in the forthcoming pantomime. The Gaumont Cinema was to remain open for another twelve years. The underground toilets can be seen in the foreground.

SECTION ONE

The End of the War

VE DAY, 8 MAY 1945 AT 3.20 P.M. ON LONG ROW, looking towards Griffin and Spalding, now Debenhams. It seemed that everyone was intent on being in the Square on that great day.

VE DAY, 1945, in the Old Market Square at 3 p.m. when Winston Churchill was broadcasting to the nation. The mood of the people was relief and joy after six years of war affecting the whole country.

AFTER LISTENING TO MR CHURCHILL'S SPEECH, the huge crowd remained in the Square for several hours and buses had great difficulty in operating. Later in the day there was a religious service, a band concert and dancing which continued until after the last buses had departed.

VE DAY AT 8.00 P.M. in the Old Market Square. The structure on the left is the indicator of the National Savings in Nottingham.

'You were barely away two hours. She's been as good as gold. The blokes at work don't believe it when I tell them how easy she is. But I reckon we're lucky, mum said she didn't get a decent night's sleep until I was two years old.'

A few moments later, with a sleepy Michelle nestled in her arms, Janie continued. 'All I found out is that Bertie Williams and Luigi's father know each other. And Luigi reckons his father sent Bertie to England to keep an eye on him.'

'It sounds odd. Luigi is hardly a teenager. It would be like Philip sending Jessica to watch out for you. Mind you, now I think about it, I suppose that's not such a bad idea,' Greg teased.

'Seriously though. I pushed him as hard as I could, but he just refused to ring his dad. What else can we do?'

'Maybe Philip can get through to him. Your dad's got a good way with most people. Or Jessica? After all, they're supposed to be friends, aren't they? Perhaps Jessica knows Luigi's father?'

For a few moments Janie was distracted by her daughter, who had started to wriggle. She moved her from one arm to the other and offered Michelle her finger to hold.

'It's so weird, Greg. Luigi turning up, then this Bertie Williams chap dying on his first day here.'

'Oh no, you don't. Don't you dare go putting your Poirot hat on. It's just one of those things. People have heart attacks. Life ends and it doesn't always end as we expect, or where we expect. I'd guess it rarely does. Come on, Michelle, give your dad a cuddle and let your mum finish her toast.'

'Your dad and Bertie are in business together?'

'No. Bertie runs a property business in and around Anzio. Renting villas out to English tourists.'

'And your father's business?

'My father runs a *successful* business empire, spreading across Italy.'

Janie didn't miss the irony in Luigi's emphasis on the word 'successful'; there was no pride in his voice, the opposite in fact. She was still trying to understand the connection between the two men; she was certain it was relevant.

'Mr Williams isn't related to you, is he?'

'No.'

'Not a kindly godfather looking out for you?' Janie's thoughts flickered to Michelle and she smiled.

'There's nothing kindly about Bertie, or my father.'

'Well, perhaps it's best you telephone your father. Let him know what's happened to his friend. He'll be able to contact Bertie's next of kin. They'll need to decide if he's to be buried here or elsewhere.'

'I have no intention of speaking to my father.'

'Luigi, I don't think you've got any choice.'

'There's always a choice.'

—

Back home, over a late breakfast, Janie recounted the morning's conversation to Greg. 'It was bizarre. I don't understand any of it and Luigi wasn't exactly forthcoming.' Janie stopped buttering her toast and stood up.

'What's the matter?'

'Did you hear Michelle? I thought I heard her just now. It's almost time for her next feed. I'll go up and fetch her, shall I? I've missed her this morning.'

VE DAY AT 8.15 P.M. in the Square. People stood and talked until late at night, when the Council House was floodlit. We had known the war in Europe was ending but there did not seem to be a quick end in sight to the war in the Far East.

AS THIS PHOTOGRAPH OF VE DAY SHOWS, the clothing of most people was becoming rather old and worn by the end of the war.

US SERVICEMEN in front of Yates's Wine Lodge in June 1944, advertising a forthcoming baseball game. The truck is the General Motors 2½ ton 6 × 6 workhorse of the US army, known as the 'Deuce-and-a-half'.

NOTTINGHAM PEOPLE crowded in front of the Council House on VJ Day, 13 August 1945, to celebrate the end of the war against Japan. The capitulation of the Japanese had come quickly following the dropping of the two atomic bombs, but the war in the Far East had not affected us directly and the general feeling was more relief than joy.

A GERMAN MIDGET SUBMARINE on display in the Square in October 1945. Unfortunately for the children who clambered over the submarine, no one was allowed inside.

THREE HUNDRED OF THESE ONE-MAN SUBMARINES, named Biber (Beaver), were put into service before the end of the war. They were not designed to be suicide weapons; torpedoes were attached to the Biber along the length of the submarine.

A DAIMLER ARMOURED CAR in the Square during 'Thanksgiving Week', October 1945. It was mounted with a two-pounder gun, a Beya machine gun and smoke dischargers.

MINE-CLEARING SHERMAN CRAB FLAIL TANK in the Square, October 1945. Sherman tanks were the most widely used mine flail tank of the Second World War. The flail was a British invention but the American Sherman tank was the preferred carrier.

VICKERS ANTI-AIRCRAFT GUN on display in the Old Market Square in April 1948. This was the QF 3.7 inch gun in its semi-mobile form. By 1941 it was the mainstay of the army's anti-aircraft defences and capable of firing a 28½ lb shell to 32,000 ft. The children in the picture appear to be in full control of the weapon.

SLC OR 'ELSIE' RADAR-CONTROLLED SEARCHLIGHT UNIT, April 1948. This strange contraption was one of the wartime inventions which was little publicized but which was very effective.

A GLOSTER METEOR F4 FIGHTER on the Goose Fair site, September 1948. The Meteor was powered by two Rolls-Royce Derwent 5 jet engines, giving a maximum speed of 580 m.p.h. Armament was 4 × 20 mm cannon.

AN AVRO LANCASTER BOMBER with white upper surfaces and black underside on the Goose Fair site. Powered by four Rolls-Royce Merlin engines, these were committed to Far East Command as part of the strategic bombing effort against Japan.

SECTION TWO

The Quincentenary

THE COUNCIL HOUSE illuminated for the Quincentenary celebrations in June 1949.

CROWDS IN THE OLD MARKET SQUARE waiting for the visit of Princess Elizabeth and the Duke of Edinburgh during the Quincentenary, June 1949. This was the first visit to Nottingham by the Princess after her marriage to Prince Philip.

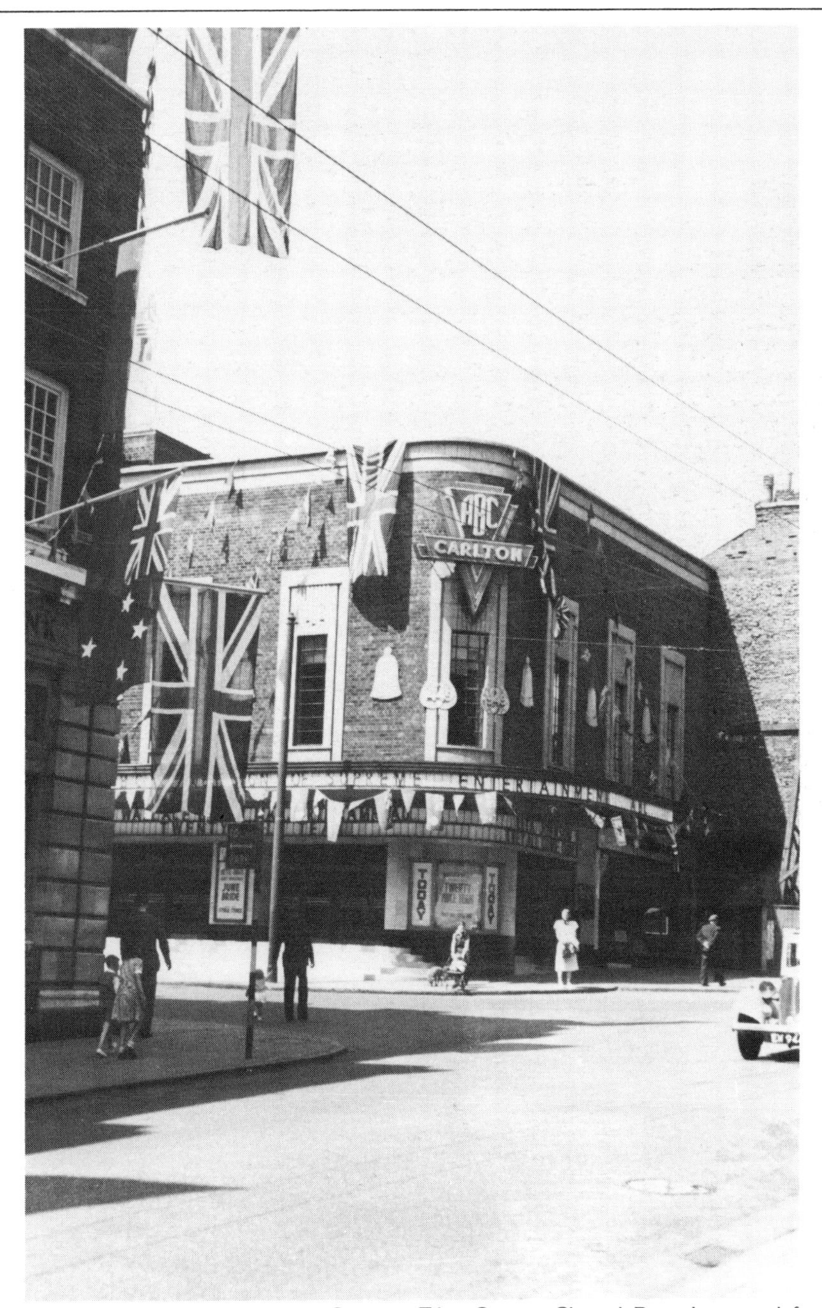

THE CARLTON CINEMA, later renamed Cannon Film Centre, Chapel Bar, decorated for the Quincentenary. This was taken in the days when cinema programmes included two feature films and a newsreel.

THE NOTTINGHAM CO-OPERATIVE SOCIETY STORE on Parliament Street, decorated for the Quincentenary. The shop was built in 1928 on the site of St George's Hall, a Victorian music hall.

DISPLAYS OF FLOWERS in front of the Council House for the Quincentenary. The girls in the foreground, apparently twins, appear to be posing for the camera.

A SOCIALIST PARADE on Long Row during the Quincentenary celebrations to commemorate 500 years since the Great Charter was granted to Nottingham. The Charter removed the borough from the authority of the high sheriff and gave to the town two sheriffs (previously bailiffs). Robin Hood was an appropriate figurehead for the parade.

ANOTHER PART OF THE PARADE through the city centre. The Chartist movement in Nottingham had celebrated their centenary in 1948 and Feargus O'Connor, its leader in 1848, had been a national figure. The Black Boy Chocolate Shop and the Mikado Restaurant on Long Row are in the background of the photograph.

THE PARADE THROUGH THE SQUARE had a political message – the van has a sign on its side giving it permission by the strike committee to proceed.

WILLIAM (WILLIE) GALLACHER, the last Communist MP in the House of Commons, speaking at a meeting in the Old Market Square during the Quincentenary in 1949.

THE AQUASTAGE BUILT ON THE RIVER TRENT for the Quincentenary was used to present concerts, pageants, and other entertainments. The building to the left is the Plaisaunce, Jesse Boot's house built at the turn of the century and demolished in 1961.

CYCLISTS IN A RACE on the Forest Recreation Ground, July 1949. In the background is a motorized invalid carriage of pre-war date.

SECTION THREE

Streets

DRURY HILL in 1968, just before the shops closed for the last time. The top of the hill was the site in the Middle Ages of the Postern Gate.

ST PETER'S SQUARE AND WHEELER GATE on a quiet Sunday in 1944. Most of these buildings have now been demolished except the Tudor style structure on the left, then occupied by Morley's Café and Paige's dress shop.

PARLIAMENT STREET in 1944. Gas Board excavations were a hazard even during the war.

WALNUT TREE LANE in August 1945 was a curving road leading down from Castle Road to Castle Boulevard. Houses were already being demolished, but it still had character. All this area was eventually flattened to make way for the People's College of Further Education and Maid Marian Way.

THE WEST BRIDGFORD SIDE of Trent Bridge in September 1946. Standing in a prominent position is the Trent Bridge Inn. This inn, built in 1885, stands on the site of William Clarke's earlier hostelry.

THE TUDOR CINEMA, Central Avenue, West Bridgford in 1952. Architecturally unique, the Tudor was built in 1931 and closed in October 1959.

A SUNDAY GRAPHIC READER on Upper Parliament Street in 1948. The building on the right is the Turkish Baths, the sauna of those days.

PRIVATE EDSON, A PRISONER OF WAR IN KOREA, receiving a hero's welcome on returning to his home in Sketchley Street in 1951.

PARLIAMENT STREET AND CHAPEL BAR in 1948. The building on the corner, occupied by Hickling's the wine merchants, was an eighteenth-century house, now sadly demolished.

CASTLE ROAD, from near the entrance to the castle, in 1949. Walnut Tree Lane is on the left and further down are Jessamine Cottages. The building on the left is part of Mortimer's House built by Watson Fothergill in 1883. Severn's Restaurant was rebuilt lower down Castle Road, and the People's College of Further Education was built in 1961 to replace St Nicholas's Church School, the steeple of which is visible on the right.

SMITHY ROW in 1952, when Burton's seemed to be a permanent fixture. Burton's was a high-class grocery store and had splendid displays of food, especially at Christmas time.

THE ENTRANCE TO VICTORIA STATION on Lower Parliament Street, the day after it closed on 18 April 1959.

WHEELER GATE in 1966. Church Street, at the side of St Peter's church, was closed and Marks and Spencer were about to expand.

HOLLOWSTONE, the old road to the south from the town, has not changed much since this photograph was taken in 1964. The houses on the right have gone but the factories remain.

DRURY HILL in 1964 was a street with a history stretching back to the Middle Ages and many interesting shops, including Higham's shoe shop, established there in 1848.

ANOTHER VIEW OF DRURY HILL. This street had character and also a noticeable smell from a leather goods shop. When the Broad Marsh Centre was built, this street was, to the great dismay of many people, replaced by an escalator.

WEEKDAY CROSS in 1964. The building on the left at the corner of Middle Pavement was demolished when Fletcher Gate was widened.

A FIRE AT CAVENDISH STORE on Long Row in 1966. The photograph shows the varied style of buildings on Long Row, old houses remaining among twentieth-century additions.

ANOTHER VIEW OF THE FIRE at the Cavendish Store. *The Sound of Music* was in the last few weeks of its extended run at the Odeon Cinema.

LONG ROW in November 1966. Prominent is the Black Boy Hotel, designed by Watson Fothergill in 1887 and enlarged in 1893 – now only a memory.

NEWTON BUILDING, part of the Technical College, dominates Goldsmith Street in December 1966. The Victorian house remains but the Royal Concert Hall has replaced the buildings in the distance.

ST JAMES'S STREET in November 1966. The Imperial is a good example of a Victorian public house and the two buildings next to it are Georgian town houses, both used as warehouses for a number of years.

A PHOTOGRAPH SHOWING THE 1888 GUILDHALL and, next to it, the construction of the new city treasury in December 1966.

CASTLE PLACE has several houses from the Georgian period and the area makes a good impression on visitors to the castle. (June 1974.)

CASTLE ROAD AND CASTLE PLACE, June 1974. Mortimer's House on the right was originally a terrace of six houses and shops. Designed by Watson Fothergill, it has a splendidly varied roofline.

ISLAND AT THE JUNCTION OF LONDON ROAD AND CANAL STREET, July 1969. St Patrick's church has since been pulled down, but Plumptre Almshouses have been left untouched.

THE OLD CORNER PIN from the Victoria Centre in 1974. This eighteenth-century public house has an interesting façade which was retained for incorporation within a shopping development in 1990.

SECTION FOUR

Shops

LISTER GATE, looking towards the Walter Fountain and Collins' Almshouses, in 1948. This is a wet Sunday morning but British Home Stores are having their windows cleaned. The Walter Fountain which had been at the junction of Greyfriar Gate and Carrington Street since 1866 was demolished in 1950.

FARMER'S DRAPERY STORE on the Poultry. This shop, which was demolished in 1974, was on the site of Thomas Smith's bank. The Flying Horse Hotel, which had a history of 500 years, is in the background. This building was converted into a shopping arcade in 1987.

PULLMAN'S STORES in 1939. This was an old-established shop which extended along almost a whole block on Lower Parliament Street.

MANSFIELD ROAD just prior to the war. The sign in the shoe shop on the right advertises men's shoes soled and heeled for 4s. 0d. and women's shoes for 2s. 6d.

SKINNER AND ROOK'S SHOP shortly after its closure in 1955. This shop was started by Mr Skinner in 1844 and he was joined by Mr Rook in 1860. This photograph was probably taken on a Sunday judging by the deserted streets.

AUSTIN REED'S men's clothing shop in Market Street in April 1950. Men dressed very formally in the 1940s and '50s, either in suits or in sports jackets and flannel trousers.

DOLCIS SHOE SHOP on Long Row in April 1950, well known for its fashionable shoes.

A FRESH FISH SHOP IN HYSON GREEN in 1953 when this type of shop was quite common. The prices for fish ranged from 1s. 6d. for kippers to 3s. 4d. for turbot. Rabbits, which were fairly cheap, were regularly eaten in those days.

THE CENTRAL MARKET at the corner of King Edward Street and Glasshouse Street, 1955. The market, which was opened in 1928, had a special character about it, and when it closed in 1972 to be incorporated within the Victoria Centre there were many protests. The building was finally demolished in 1985.

FRIAR LANE AND WHEELER GATE CORNER in 1960. The Oriental Café was a splendid building, with a fine carved ceiling which was fortunately saved when the building was demolished. The ceiling has since been re-sited in Holme Pierrepont Hall.

THE OLD PAINTED SIGN above these doors in Cliff Road in 1964 advertises lodgings. Double beds were 6d. according to the sign, which was still visible until 1990.

SHOPPERS ON LONG ROW in December 1966. The display in Griffin and Spalding's window reflects the season.

ST JAMES'S STREET in April 1973, a narrow street which has still not been widened although it has been cut in half by Maid Marian Way. The Old Malt Cross music hall occupied the building on the right.

SECTION FIVE

Boots the Chemists

BOOTS DAY AND NIGHT BRANCH in Wheeler Gate, April 1950 was – like the Windmill Theatre in London – an institution. The shop was opened in 1917 and extended in 1933 before finally closing in 1962.

BOOTS FACTORIES in London Road in 1939. These buildings are still used as warehouses by Boots. The high-level railway station holds memories for many Nottingham people.

A VISIT TO BOOTS BY KING GEORGE VI AND QUEEN ELIZABETH in March 1943. In the group with the Queen are, from left to right: the equerry to the King, Dr P.C. Brett, Mr B.A. Bull, Mr J.P. Savage, Mr H.S. Hibbins, Mr L. Anderson and Mr E.L.B. Thomas.

A DISPLAY OF BOOTS GARDENING PRODUCTS at the Astoria Cinema, Lenton, part of the presentation by Mr C.H. Middleton, the BBC gardening expert of the 1930s and '40s.

BOOTS FACTORIES IN ISLAND STREET, June 1969. These factories were among the first used by Jesse Boot for the manufacture of medicines and toiletries.

GIRLS LEARNING NEEDLEWORK at Boots College, formerly Boots Day Continuation School, in 1944. Young employees were given tuition on one day a week in a variety of subjects including art, music, English literature, French, cookery and dancing. The college closed after fifty years, in 1969.

THE TYPISTS' TRAINING DEPARTMENT of Boots in 1957. This department gave thirty weeks' training in shorthand and typewriting to young employees. The teacher is Mrs Margaret Phillips.

GIRLS BEING TAUGHT SHORTHAND by Miss Margaret Bell in Boots Typists' Training Department in 1957. The office was in Lawrence's Building next to the railway bridge on Station Street and classes were frequently disrupted by trains rumbling past.

MRS MARGARET WHITWORTH teaching the shorthand class in Boots Typists' Training Department in 1970. The department moved along with the general offices from Station Street to the Beeston site in 1968.

BOOTS GENERAL OFFICES in Station Street after their closure in March 1968. This building was Hine & Mundella's factory until 1912 when Jesse Boot bought it. Jesse Boot's office was on the first floor over the main entrance.

BOOTS SHOP IN HIGH STREET in 1946. This shop was Jesse Boot's pride and joy and set the standard for his other town centre stores. This branch closed in May 1972.

BOOTS WHEELER GATE BRANCH, with its 1930s façade, in 1948. The shop was open continuously until 1962, when the business was moved to new premises nearer Friar Lane.

BOOTS THE CHEMISTS SHOP in Lister Gate in 1960. This shop was typical of the hundreds of smaller Boots shops throughout the country at this period – they carried a great variety and number of products. It closed in November 1962.

BOOTS BRANCH NO. 2 at Trent Bridge in March 1965. The branch was built in Tudor style and was finally closed as a shop in April 1969. The building continues to be used by Boots as a Social Club. Trolley bus wires have been re-touched from the sky but are still visible in front of the chimneys.

THE BOOTS BRANCH ON PARLIAMENT STREET in 1970. This branch preceded the present Victoria Centre branch.

SECTION SIX

Buildings

AN INSURANCE COMPANY SIGN in Low Pavement, September 1946. The sign is on an eighteenth-century building at the corner of Bridlesmith Gate.

THE BLACK BOY HOTEL, Long Row, February 1952. This hotel was built on land leased from Brunts' Charity and when the lease expired in 1969 it was closed, to be replaced by Littlewoods' store. The hotel was a famous landmark and much loved by Nottingham people.

PLUMPTRE ALMSHOUSES in Poplar Street, 1955. The almshouses were founded in 1392 by John Plumptre; the present building dates from 1823.

THE GARDEN OF COLLINS' ALMSHOUSES in Friar Lane, 1955, an oasis in the centre of the city. Regrettably, the almshouses were demolished when the area was cleared in 1956 to build Maid Marian Way.

THIS BUILDING has had a varied history since it opened as Pringle's Picture Palace in 1911. After a period as the Goldsmith Picture House, it became the Repertory Theatre in 1942 and later still the Little Theatre before becoming the first Nottingham Playhouse.

THE TURKISH BATHS AND ODD HOUR CINEMA just before their demolition in 1962. The Turkish Baths were by then becoming outdated and the Odd Hour Cinema, previously the News Theatre, had also become redundant.

THE GLOBE BINGO HALL, formerly the Globe Cinema, Trent Bridge, after its closure in 1961. The cinema opened in 1912 but suffered from the competition of television in the 1950s.

ST NICHOLAS'S CHURCH SCHOOL at the corner of Castle Road and Mortimer Street in 1952. This school, which was built in 1859, was closed in 1912 but was not demolished until 1956.

THE SHIRE HALL in 1966. Built in 1788, it was used as a courthouse for 200 years, but since its closure the future of the Shire Hall has been in doubt.

A WEA CLASS in one of the courts in the Shire Hall, 1971. When this building was part of the county, it was claimed to be the smallest parish in the country.

BROAD MARSH, 1940. The demolition of the back-to-back houses began in the 1930s and the opportunity was taken to a stage a mock air-raid to test the city's civil defence services.

BROAD MARSH in 1959, when the area was almost cleared. The railway line was still in use – the arches underneath were to be used for another thirty years.

A TEMPORARY CHANGE OF USE for Broad Marsh, 1966. During the 1960s the area was used as a bus station and car park.

THE HIGH PAVEMENT UNITARIAN CHURCH dominates the skyline in April 1968. In the 1980s the church's steeple was removed as it was unsafe. It was then rebuilt before the building was finally reopened as the city's Lace Hall.

HOLY TRINITY CHURCH just before the war. The steeple was removed in 1941 owing to bomb damage, but the church remained for another seventeen years, eventually to be replaced by a car park in 1958.

THE BUILDING ON THE LEFT was John Player's factory in Broad Marsh where, in 1877, he took over the tobacco business begun in 1823 by William Wright. These buildings were demolished in 1968.

OLD PEVEREL OR DEBTORS' PRISON, St Peter's Street, Radford in April 1968 just before its demolition. This eighteenth-century building was originally a workhouse and when the premises were vacated in 1790 the building was used as a prison for debtors sued in the Court of Honour of Peverel. In those days no provision was made for feeding the prisoners, who were dependent on charity, and consequently their condition was often pitiful. The powers of the court ceased in 1849 and the property was then used as two cottages.

NEWDIGATE HOUSE, CASTLE GATE in 1964. The area was being cleared for the first stage of Nottingham's inner ring road. Fortunately this splendid house was saved.

CASTLE GATE, May 1971. A group of eighteenth-century houses which have been restored and are now used as the Costume Museum and the Leisure Services Arts Department.

NEWDIGATE HOUSE in 1967, after its restoration. It is now the home of the Nottingham and Notts. United Services Club after their move from Maypole Yard. It is one of the most handsome buildings in Nottingham and has a famous history, being the house in which Marshal Tallard was kept after his capture at the Battle of Blenheim in 1704.

THE REMAINS OF BOBBERS MILL in April 1968. This mill, which was built *c.* 1800, was one of several on the banks of the River Leen.

WILLIAM BOOTH'S BIRTHPLACE in 1966. This house, in which Booth was born in 1829, was bought by the Salvation Army prior to the war and incorporated into a Goodwill Centre in 1971.

THE EMPIRE THEATRE, which was built in 1898 and closed in 1958. The Empire was demolished in 1969 to make way for the Royal Concert Hall.

THE ENTRANCE TO MAYPOLE YARD at the side of the Black Boy Hotel, June 1969. The statue on the façade is of Samuel Brunt. This was removed to East Bridgford parish church when the hotel was pulled down.

SEVERN'S RESTAURANT on Middle Pavement in August 1963. This small structure was a typical fifteenth-century house and was named after the wine merchants who also occupied the adjoining Georgian house.

THE EXCAVATIONS IN PARK ROW in August 1963 when Maid Marian Way was being constructed. The excavations revealed parts of the old town wall.

SEVERN'S RESTAURANT, MIDDLE PAVEMENT being pulled down in 1969 before being rebuilt on Castle Road. The wooden structure of the building is clearly visible.

ANOTHER PHOTOGRAPH OF SEVERN'S BEING PULLED DOWN. Fortunately, this demolition had a happy ending and the building was saved.

THE TRIP TO JERUSALEM public house, June 1974. In all probability there has been an ale-house on this site since the Middle Ages, but the present building dates mainly from the seventeenth century.

VICTORIA RAILWAY STATION in 1965 towards the end of its life; it closed in 1967. The Victoria Station, like the Midland Station, was designed by A.E. Lambert, but had more atmosphere.

THE VICTORIA CLOCK TOWER in April 1973, dwarfed by the Victoria Centre flats. The two together make a complete contrast in architectural styles. The tower and Victoria Station Hotel, now Stakis Victoria Hotel, are all that are left to remind us of the Victoria railway station.

AN UNUSUAL VIEW OF THE VICTORIA CLOCK TOWER in April 1973. This photograph, taken from the roof of the Victoria Centre flats, provides a new angle on the remaining part of the Victoria railway station.

SECTION SEVEN

Old Market Square

VIEW FROM THE STEPS of the Council House, November 1966. The stone lions flanking the entrance to the Council House have been a rendezvous for countless people over the years.

THE FOUNTAINS in the Old Market Square in 1939. The Old Moot Hall can be seen in the background. During the war the fountains were replaced by National Fire Service water tanks, but fire precautions were unable to save the Moot Hall which received a direct hit from a high explosive bomb during the blitz in May 1941.

THE SWITCHING-ON OF THE CHRISTMAS LIGHTS, 1949. With only the floodlit Council House as background, this was a very attractive scene.

THE STATUE OF QUEEN VICTORIA, which faced the Council House from 1905 to 1953 when it was removed to the Memorial Gardens by the River Trent.

AN ARTIST in the Old Market Square, September 1946. Subjects for artists and photographers have always abounded here.

WINTER SUNSHINE on the cobbles of Beastmarket Hill in January 1947. Fifty Shilling Tailors are on the right – they had to change their name after many years, when inflation took over. At King's Restaurant, business men and shoppers took coffee in the mornings and, later on, tea and cakes were served.

AN EARNEST DISCUSSION in April 1948 between Mr Stone, with his back to the camera, a regular speaker in the Old Market Square, and a group of Mormons.

ANOTHER STUDY IN EXPRESSIONS in the Old Market Square. Although St Peter's Square has taken away some of the orators, the Square still attracts groups like this.

THE FRONT OF THE COUNCIL HOUSE, April 1953. Women shoppers were in the majority in the centre of the city in the 1940s and '50s.

A BUSY SCENE ON LONG ROW, Christmas 1966. Through traffic was still allowed into the centre of the city in those days.

THE OLD MARKET SQUARE, December 1966, in the years when the Christmas tree was the only decoration in the Square.

ANOTHER PICTURE OF THE SQUARE in December 1966. The crane on Market Square House is rising above the skyline during the construction of the building.

YATES'S WINE LODGE on Long Row, December 1966. This wine lodge with its Victorian bar and gallery is a popular attraction and recent alterations and restorations have fortunately been carried out with sensitivity.

THE CROSSING TOWARDS GRIFFIN & SPALDING (now Debenhams), full of purposeful women shoppers, just before Christmas 1966.

THE BLACK BOY HOTEL in December 1966. This was the hotel where the Australian cricket team stayed whenever they played at Trent Bridge – the English team stayed at the Victoria Station Hotel.

SOUTH PARADE AND THE OLD MARKET SQUARE, December 1966. The Square was the only venue for soap box orators at that time, but this audience was rather thin and inattentive.

MARKET SQUARE HOUSE in November 1967. It replaced an earlier structure which had been built in more traditional style. The new building unfortunately dominates the western end of the Square.

THE OLD MARKET SQUARE from the balcony of the Council House in May 1973. There have been plans over the years to change the Square but, other than an alteration of the skyline, it has changed little in the past sixty years.

WHATEVER THE MERITS OF THE MARKET SQUARE HOUSE, the view from the top floor is well worth seeing. This June 1969 photograph shows the splendid city centre with the skyline broken only by the dome of the Council House. The Black Boy Hotel and Farmer's store can also be seen.

LONG ROW in June 1969, showing the mixture of architectural styles. The colonnades, a feature of the Row for the past 300 years, have been retained and are invaluable in wet weather.

THE COUNCIL HOUSE in June 1969, from the Pearl Assurance Building. This view shows how dominant the Council House was before the multi-storey buildings were erected in the city centre.

GRIFFIN & SPALDING (now Debenhams) have been on their present site for over a hundred years, expanding from a small draper's shop situated at the corner of Sheep Lane in 1865. The skyline is broken by the Newton Building, part of the Technical College.

THE FOUNTAINS WERE RESTORED to the Old Market Square after the war. The Royal Air Force display in the background of this May 1973 photograph includes a Red Arrow aeroplane.

ONE OF THE EARLIER NOTTINGHAM FESTIVALS which have enlivened the city and become very popular, being both cultural and entertaining.

SECTION EIGHT

Goose Fair

GALLOPING HORSES at the Goose Fair in October 1947 – a stately ride to judge by the expression on the face of the woman in the foreground.

THE CHILDRENS' SECTION OF THE GOOSE FAIR, October 1947. In the daytime this part of the fair is always the busiest.

THE FRONT OF A SHOW which is exhibiting 'The horse with the human brain'. The attractions appeared more exciting from outside the booths than was the reality.

SPEEDWAY CARS at the Goose Fair in October 1947. The speedway and dodgem cars have been a popular attraction at the fair for years. In the background is one of the entrances from Gregory Boulevard.

GOOSE FAIR AT NIGHT. The big wheel is another ride which has retained its popularity for many years.

CHILDRENS' WHEEL, October 1947. The wheel went high enough to give a view without upsetting the young passengers too much.

THE DOUBLE BIG WHEEL at the fair in October 1947. Not the biggest of wheels but still high enough to give a thrill.

A GENERAL SCENE at the Goose Fair in 1951. The rides look dated now but they thrilled their patrons as much as the modern ones do today.

THE CONSTRUCTION OF THE GOOSE FAIR in 1951. The showmen are allowed onto the site on the Monday before the Goose Fair starts and in three days they build one of the biggest fairs in the country.

A ROCKET ROUNDABOUT, in which the riders could alter the height of their flight, at the fair in 1951.

AFTERNOON SUNSHINE at the Goose Fair makes a picture of patterns on the roundabout. Youths looking for female companions are a familiar sight at the fair.

THE DEPARTURE OF THE FIRST GOOSE FAIR after the war, October 1945. Scavenging on the Forest after the fair had ended was a new experience for the many youths who had cycled there. The pre-war bus in the middle of the picture appears to have been converted to run on gas.

SECTION NINE

River Trent and Floods

A VIEW FROM TRENT BRIDGE towards the Suspension Bridge on a sunny afternoon in September 1946. In this picture the trees in Lover's Walk are still standing.

A FREQUENT SIGHT on the River Trent: rowing crews being coached by a cyclist riding along the river bank.

ONE OF THE MOTOR LAUNCHES on the River Trent returning from a cruise in August 1946. Excursions were occasionally made to Gunthorpe and Newark, giving two hours ashore.

A YACHT WITH ITS MAST LOWERED cruising under Trent Bridge in June 1947. The chow on deck seems very composed.

SAILING CABIN CRUISERS moored at Radcliffe-on-Trent in August 1945. Petrol was still rationed and sails for boats were essential.

A RACING ROWING BOAT on the flooded River Trent near the Suspension Bridge, February 1946.

A SINGLE SCULLER near Trent Bridge in 1951. The Town Arms public house is in the background.

A CABIN CRUISER which was swept over Colwick Weir in August 1947. This stretch of the River Trent was very hazardous but has now been straightened and channelled through new locks.

FLOODS ON VICTORIA EMBANKMENT, February 1946. This photograph was taken from the Suspension Bridge and shows the river at almost record levels and twice its normal width.

CARS RUNNING THROUGH FLOODS on Trent Boulevard, West Bridgford in February 1946. Most cars on the road at this time were pre-war models which had been stored through the war.

INHABITANTS OF THE MEADOWS being carried to dry land on a corporation dumper during the floods of March 1947. A scene in Kirkewhite Street at the corner of Cremorne Street.

FLOODS ON ALBERT ROAD, West Bridgford in March 1947. Most cars managed to get through the water although some drivers had problems when their car engines flooded. The Tudor Cinema is visible in the background.

LORRIES BEING DRIVEN THROUGH FLOODS near the park on Albert Road, West Bridgford, March 1947.

FLOODS AT THE JUNCTION OF LOUGHBOROUGH ROAD AND RADCLIFFE ROAD in West Bridgford, February 1946. On the left of the picture is the police house which was built in 1847 and is now demolished.

A HOUSEWIFE GOES SHOPPING along Wilford Road by Clyde Street in the floods of March 1947.

NOTTINGHAM FOREST FOOTBALL GROUND in the floods of March 1947. During this period Nottingham Forest played their home games at Notts. County's ground in Meadow Lane.

FLOODS ON RADFORD ROAD in 1953 after a cloudburst. Trolley buses managed to operate with difficulty but, fortunately, these scenes were very rare.

FLOODS AT WILFORD near the Ferry Inn in December 1960. In the background is the North Wilford power station, demolition of which began in 1983 and was completed in 1987.

THE *BALLERINA* brings back the Reverend Arthur H. Bird and the party from Bridgway Hall Methodist Church after he had conducted a riverside service in July 1955. In the background is the Plaza Cinema, built on the site of the Nottingham Industrial Exhibition (opened in 1903 and burnt down in 1904). The cinema, originally named the Pavilion, became the Trent Bridge Palace Theatre in 1927 and in 1932 opened as the Plaza Cinema, finally closing at the beginning of the war. The building was demolished in 1961 to make way for the Bridgford Hotel.

A SCENE ON THE RIVER TRENT which has changed very little over the years – rowing boats are still for hire and swans are eager to be fed. The trees in Lovers' Walk confirm this photograph was taken before 1951.

THE *PRIDE OF THE YARE* on the River Trent in 1951. This boat, which was on the Norfolk Broads before the war, was one of the small vessels which helped to ferry troops back from Dunkirk in 1940.

CLIFTON BRIDGE UNDER CONSTRUCTION in 1956. Nottingham had needed another road bridge over the River Trent for some years and this bridge was opened in February 1958.

THIS PHOTOGRAPH, taken in 1956, shows how Clifton Bridge was constructed. Because of the volume of traffic a second bridge was needed, and this was built alongside the first in 1971/2.

THE SUSPENSION BRIDGE over the River Trent in September 1946. This bridge was built in 1906 to carry foot passengers between West Bridgford and Nottingham.

THE WILFORD TOLL BRIDGE in 1972. The building of the bridge commenced in 1863 but it was not officially opened until 1870. The bridge was closed to cars in 1974 as it was unsafe and closed to all traffic in 1981.

THE WILFORD TOLL BRIDGE AND THE GREAT CENTRAL RAILWAY BRIDGE in 1972. The last train crossed the railway bridge in 1969 but foot passengers made temporary use of it while the toll bridge was being rebuilt in 1981/2.

TOLL BRIDGE LODGE in 1972, now converted into a newsagent's shop. The board displaying the tolls remains but the printing has faded.

SECTION TEN

Sport and Pastimes

CHICK ZAMICK FACING-OFF for Nottingham Panthers in an ice hockey match against Wembley Monarchs in December 1947. In the late 1940s ice hockey became very popular in Nottingham. Zamick was a prolific goal scorer for the Panthers.

DURING AND FOLLOWING THE WAR 'Holidays-at-Home' were encouraged. This is a fair which was held in Bridgford Park, West Bridgford in August 1945.

CYCLISTS ON VICTORIA EMBANKMENT on a sunny afternoon in October 1945. The embankment was built in 1901 and landscaped in the 1920s thanks to the generosity of Jesse Boot. It has been a favourite spot for Nottingham people ever since.

HIGHFIELDS LIDO was a popular resort, particularly in the years immediately after the war when holidays-at-home were common. The water in this August 1947 photograph does not appear to have been very warm as there are more people around the pool than in it. The lido was opened in August 1924, at the same time as the University Park was laid out, and closed in 1981.

THREE SWIMMERS making a novel entrance into the water at Highfields Lido.

ANOTHER SWIMMER TAKING THE PLUNGE at Highfields in October 1947.

THE BOATING LAKE on the South Shore at Skegness – Nottingham-by-the-Sea – in September 1948. The east coast was still the favourite holiday destination for the majority of Nottingham people well into the 1950s.

HIGH JUMPER ON THE FOREST RECREATION GROUND, taking part in a sports event held there in July 1949.

MINIATURE YACHT CHAMPIONSHIP on Highfields Lake. The men standing in the water, with boats taller than themselves, seem to be receiving their orders from the starter.

TWO BOYS WITH A FISHING NET in the River Leen. The stream is clearly shallow but the Leen often overflowed its banks and flooded nearby houses.

NOTTINGHAMSHIRE AND SUSSEX CRICKETERS leaving the field at Trent Bridge in August 1949. Among the Notts. players are Reg Simpson, Joe Hardstaff, Walter Keeton and Harold Butler.

HARRY WALKER SAVING FOR NOTTINGHAM FOREST in a second division game against Chesterfield at the City Ground in October 1948.

A PRACTICE MATCH before the start of the season at Meadow Lane, August 1948. The appearance of Tommy Lawton, third from right, ensured that all keen Notts. County supporters would attend the match.

A FRIENDLY MATCH between Notts. County and Clyde in May 1950 – Notts. County defending. In the Lawton era, Notts. County attracted good attendances, even for friendly matches.

NOTTINGHAM FOREST FOOTBALL CLUB in the 1956/7 season, when the club was promoted to the first division. Billy Walker sitting at the left, was the manager, a position he held for twenty-one years until 1960.

NOTTS. COUNTY FOOTBALL CLUB in the 1956/7 season, managed by George Poyser, sitting centre front.

SECTION ELEVEN

Transport

BARTON'S TRANSPORT BOOKING OFFICE in Huntingdon Street in July 1947 – a typical 1930s building.

A ROBIN HOOD BUS pulling out of Taddington on the Blackpool to Nottingham route in July 1946. These were the latest luxury coaches.

A BARTON'S BUS on an attractive stretch of road near Keyworth, March 1946. Haystacks had a traditional shape in those days.

A LAGONDA CAR, which would be a classic today, appears to be stranded in a field near Holme Pierrepont church, March 1947.

AN ARMSTRONG SIDDELEY CAR in Chapel Bar, August 1947. This car was very eye-catching and had American styling. Across the street was Henry Barker's store which had very unusual convex windowpanes.

A HORSE-DRAWN BUS in Greyfriar Gate in April 1948, borrowed from the Leicester Corporation for the Golden Jubilee of the Nottingham Corporation Transport Department. The bus travelled along Castle Boulevard from the city centre for a 1s. 0d. fare. The dray horse on the left was one of a dwindling number of working horses on Nottingham roads.

SHIPSTONE'S DRAY HORSES, photographed in April 1968, made a splendid sight on Nottingham's roads and they were used for publicity purposes long after the need for them had passed. Scotholme public house, at the corner of Radford Road and Gladstone Street, was one of the many Shipstone houses in the city.

THE TYPE OF TRANSPORT which gradually replaced Shipstone's dray horses and carts. Philip Shipley, on the left, and his mate Len Blake are unloading their Foden's lorry in 1949.

DELIVERY VANS OF J. HARDY & CO. LTD in Tattershall Drive in The Park in April 1951. The Park was laid out by T.C. Hine in a series of crescents and circles, but for strangers it can be confusing.

THE RAILWAY GOODS YARD from London Road during the floods of March 1947. Trains continued to run even in almost impossible conditions.

A TRAIN PULLING INTO RADFORD STATION during the floods of March 1947. The overflowing of the River Leen was a regular occurrence in the 1940s.

THE MIDLAND STATION during the floods of March 1947. The locomotive and carriages just cleared the water but their speed was dead slow in order to avoid disturbing the water.

PLATFORM 5 AT THE MIDLAND STATION in 1946. This picture evokes another age and could be a scene from *Brief Encounter*. The locomotive appears to have seen better days.

VICTORIA RAILWAY STATION in November 1955. This station, opened on 24 May 1900, was originally to be called the Great Central and Great Northern Joint Nottingham station but sense prevailed and, as the date of the opening was Queen Victoria's birthday, it was renamed in her honour. The building on the left is the Mechanics Institute, rebuilt in 1869 after a fire had almost completely burnt down the previous hall.

A PHOTOGRAPH CAPTURING THE ATMOSPHERE OF VICTORIA STATION, the favourite station of many Nottingham people.

THREE LOCOMOTIVES SENDING SMOKE AND STEAM INTO THE AIR at Victoria station in 1951. This was a common sight in those days but railway enthusiasts would now travel miles to see such a scene.

THE FOOTBRIDGE AT VICTORIA STATION in 1951. Everyone seems to have a purposeful step and to be unaware of the photographer composing his picture of light and shade.

SECTION TWELVE

Views

VIEW FROM THE CASTLE GROUNDS in August 1949 towards the city centre, then unspoilt by the multi-storey car parks and office blocks which have since been built.

THE LANE TO THE FOURTEENTH-CENTURY STRELLEY CHURCH in March 1946. This view has changed little in the past forty-five years although major roads have since been built within a half a mile of this scene.

VILLAGE ROAD, CLIFTON in June 1945. Unlike the view of Strelley above, this scene has changed considerably and Clifton has lost much of its rural character.

THE CASTLE GROUNDS in August 1949 – an oasis for office workers. The castle is a popular tourist attraction, although the renaissance building is a disappointment for those expecting a Norman castle.

PHOTOGRAPH OF THE MEADOWS FROM THE CASTLE in August 1949. The Viyella factory in the foreground, which was a pre-war modernistic building, has been converted into offices.

THE JUNCTION OF LONDON ROAD AND CANAL STREET in 1939. New Council houses replace the back-to-back houses in Narrow Marsh, and behind them Solaris' ice works can be seen.

ST PATRICK'S CHURCH from Malin Hill in 1939. Also in the photograph are Boots factories in Island Street, since rebuilt.

A VIEW FROM THE CASTLE over the People's College of Further Education in 1966. This was taken before the building of Maid Marian Way and the Broad Marsh Centre. The Electricity showroom, previously James' store, is on Carrington Street and, further away, the gas holder on Manvers Street is visible.

VIEW OF ST PETER'S CHURCH AND WHEELER GATE from the top of the Pearl Assurance Building in Friar Lane in June 1968. Also in the picture is the spire of High Pavement church and the tower of St Mary's church.

A PHOTOGRAPH OF WHEELER GATE taken from Market Square House in June 1969, showing the Victorian façades to the buildings on the left and, from this viewpoint, the prominence of the three churches.

A VIEW FROM THE PEARL ASSURANCE BUILDING in June 1968, showing the new approach to the castle.

VIEW OF THE LACE MARKET in July 1969, showing the factories on Hollowstone and Malin Hill immediately below them.

MANSFIELD ROAD in 1973. The Rose of England public house (now named the Yorker), built by Watson Fothergill in 1899, is in the foreground.

THE PARLIAMENT STREET METHODIST CHURCH is on the right of this April 1973 photograph and, further away, the Lace Market can be seen.

A VIEW TOWARDS THE CITY CENTRE from the top of the Victoria Centre flats in April 1973. The Council House is prominent and in the distance are the chimneys of the North Wilford power station.

LOOKING NORTH FROM THE VICTORIA CENTRE FLATS in April 1973. The building in the middle of the picture is York House, headquarters of Radio Nottingham and East Midlands Television. The entrance to the Sherwood railway tunnel is on the right, evidence of the enormous amount of labour involved in building the Great Central railway line.

A SIMILAR VIEWPOINT TO THE LAST PHOTOGRAPH, but looking south. The Central Market is immediately below and the buildings of the Lace Market are in the middle distance.

ACKNOWLEDGEMENTS

I would like to thank Chris Weir of the Nottinghamshire Archives Office, who encouraged me to produce this book, and Clive Hardy, Nigel Arthur and Ralph Gee for their help and support. I would also like to express my appreciation to the following for their permission to reproduce photographs:

Mrs May Sentance,
John Lock,
T. Bailey Forman Ltd,
Boots Museum,
The Boots Co. PLC,
Nottinghamshire Local Studies Library,
John Shipley,
R.J. Varley.

My thanks are also due to Sheila Cooke and the staff of the Nottinghamshire Local Studies Library for their unfailing kindness and help.